SPEAKEASY COCKTAILS

An Hachette UK Company
www.hachette.co.uk

First published in Great Britain in 2024 by Hamlyn, an imprint of
Octopus Publishing Group Ltd
Carmelite House
50 Victoria Embankment
London EC4Y 0DZ
www.octopusbooks.co.uk

Distributed in the US by
Hachette Book Group
1290 Avenue of the Americas
4th and 5th Floors
New York, NY 10104

Distributed in Canada by
Canadian Manda Group
664 Annette St.
Toronto, Ontario, Canada M6S 2C8

ISBN 978-0-6006-3847-6

A CIP catalogue record for this book is available from the British Library.

Printed and bound in China
10 9 8 7 6 5 4 3 2 1

Publisher: Lucy Pessell
Designer: Isobel Platt
Editor: Feyi Oyesanya
Assistant Editor: Samina Rahman

Cover illustration: This cover has been designed using assets from Freepik.com
Picture Credits: iStock: Aamulya 37, AlexPro9500 83, bhofack2 6, 13, 15, 17, 23, 33, 43,
45, 47, 49, 55, 63, 67, 75, 85, etorres69 73, 73, ivanmateev 31, Mario Marquardt Jr 51,
maurese 81, MaximFesenko 53, Mindstyle 25, perfect loop 39, timnewman 35, viennetta
57, Wirestock 27

SPEAKEASY COCKTAILS

50

CLASSIC COCKTAILS

FROM THE DECADES OF DECADENCE

SCOTT ROBERTSON

hamlyn

Algonquin	87	Journalist	21
Americano	14	Luigi	29
Aviation	66	Maiden's Blush	65
Bees Knees	44	Manhattan	16
Blinker	86	Martinez	12
Blood and Sand	82	Mint Julep	84
Bobby Burns	32	Monkey Gland	46
Boulevardier	52	Negroni	50
Boxcar	69	Old Pal	54
Bronx	30	Opera	71
Bucks Fizz	60	Paradise	78
Churchill Martini	76	Perfect Lady	70
Clover Club	22	Pink Gin	10
Corpse Reviver No. 2	26	Queen Mother	77
Death in the Afternoon	59	Satan's Whiskers	68
Dirty Martini	74	Sidecar	56
French 75	36	Singapore Sling	38
Gibson Martini	72	Southside	41
Gimlet	42	Stinger	80
Gin and It	11	The Fix	9
Gin Rickey	20	Tom Collins	24
Golden Dawn	79	Turf Club	18
Hangman's Blood	61	White Lady	34
Hanky Panky	48	Yale	19
Hemingway Daiquiri	58	Zombie	62

CONTENTS

INTRODUCTION 7

1800S 8

1900-1920 28

1920S 40

1930S 64

BAR BASICS 88

A NOTE ON MEASURES

INTRODUCTION

While much of Western society was enjoying the decadence of the Roaring Twenties, or the *années folles* ('crazy years') as they were known in France, the Prohibition era began in America.

The 18th amendment to the US constitution banned the manufacture, sale and import or export of 'intoxicating liquors' but in response, there was a proliferation of bootleggers and smugglers, individuals making 'moonshine' in their bathtubs, and 'speakeasies' or illicit bars.

Many of the cocktails of the Prohibition era were inspired by those of pre-Prohibition, but the dubious moonshine whiskies and gins had to be masked with citrus and fruit juices, ginger ales, colas and other flavours.

The result? Some of the most-loved and enduring classic cocktails that we enjoy today.

Here's a collection of 50 recipes that brings together the drinks that inspired the speakeasy classics, the drinks of the Prohibition era, and those that they in turn inspired well into the 1930s.

Cheers!

1800s

THE FIX

2 measures gin

1 measure lemon juice

¾ measure sugar syrup

seasonal fruit, to garnish

Y

Add the ingredients to a rocks
glass filled with crushed ice.

Churn, and garnish with seasonal
fruit of your choosing.

*The simplest of sours, and really the very building
blocks of all drinks making – first recorded in Jerry
Thomas's How to Mix Drinks (1862).*

PINK GIN

2 measures gin
5 dashes Angostura bitters
still water, to top

Υ

Add all the ingredients to an old
fashioned glass filled with cubed
ice and stir briefly.

No garnish.

*The 'pink gin' on today's shop shelves is a sugary, fruity affair
and not at all like the original. Vastly popular in its day,
Pink gin was conceived by naval officers in Plymouth in the
mid 1800s as a means of making a tonic prescribed for sea
sickness more palatable – that tonic was none other than
Angostura bitters. It's as bracing as a howling sou'westerly
and really does shiver the timbers. But in the best of ways.*

GIN AND IT

1 ½ measures gin
1 ½ measures Italian
sweet vermouth
orange, to garnish

Y

Add all the ingredients to a rocks
glass filled with cubed ice, stir
briefly and garnish with an
orange slice.

Meaning 'gin and Italian vermouth', despite the
simplicity of the recipe, this is a superbly complex
blend of botanical, woody and floral notes.

MARTINEZ

2 measures gin
1 measure sweet vermouth
1 teaspoon Maraschino
2 dashes Angostura bitters
orange, to garnish

$\curlyvee$

Add all the ingredients to a
cocktail shaker filled with
cubed ice.

Stir for 30 seconds, and strain into
a chilled coupette glass.

Garnish with an orange twist.

*Conceived around 1870 in Northern California,
this is a sweeter and more complex precursor to
the Martini. Stunning.*

AMERICANO

1 measure Campari
1 measure sweet vermouth
soda water, to top
orange slice, to garnish

Y

Fill a highball glass with cubed
ice, add the Campari and sweet
vermouth, stir and top with
soda water.

Garnish with an orange slice.

*Predating the Negroni, the Americano is the most classic
of Italian aperitivos. Halfway between a spritz and a
Collins, its relatively low potency means that three or four
can be enjoyed in one sitting. Simple and timeless.*

MANHATTAN

2 measures rye whiskey
1 measure sweet vermouth
2 dashes Angostura bitters
cocktail cherry, to garnish

Y

Add all the ingredients to a
cocktail shaker filled with
cubed ice.

Stir for 30 seconds, and strain into
a chilled coupette glass.

Garnish with a cocktail cherry.

*The rich wine notes from sweet vermouth, combined with
the spice and punch of rye whiskey give the drink such
depth and complexity. Stirred down and meaningful.*

TURF CLUB

1 ½ measures gin
1 ½ measures sweet vermouth
¼ measure Maraschino
1 dash absinthe
1 dash orange bitters
cocktail cherry, to garnish

Υ

Add all the ingredients to a
cocktail shaker filled with
cubed ice.

Stir for 30 seconds, and strain into
a chilled cocktail glass.

Garnish with a cocktail cherry.

*This Harry Johnson classic is a Martinez of sorts,
with a brightening splash of Maraschino.*

YALE

2 measures gin
¾ measure dry vermouth
2 tablespoons Maraschino
2 dashes orange bitters
lemon, to garnish

Y

Add all the ingredients to a
cocktail shaker filled with
cubed ice.

Stir for 30 seconds, and strain into
a chilled cocktail glass.

Garnish with a lemon twist.

*The touch of Maraschino brings an astringent, fruited
complexity. The recipe has evolved over the years with the
original calling for Crème Yvette (no longer produced)
which would have given the drink a slightly blueish hue
as a nod to Yale's colours.*

GIN RICKEY

2 measures gin
¾ measure lime juice
½ measure sugar syrup
soda water, to top
lime, to garnish

Y

Build all the ingredients in a
large wine glass full of cubed ice,
stir briefly and garnish with
a lime wedge.

Hailing from late 19th century America, the 'Rickey'
(F Scott Fitzgerald's favourite cocktail) is best described
as a 'Collins' with lime juice instead of lemon. The most
simple and delicious of gin highballs.

JOURNALIST

2 measures gin

½ measure dry vermouth

½ measure sweet vermouth

1 teaspoon lemon juice

2 dashes Angostura bitters

2 dashes orange bitters

lemon, to garnish

🍸

Add all the ingredients to a
cocktail shaker filled with
cubed ice.

Stir for 30 seconds, and strain into
a coupette cocktail glass. Garnish
with a lemon twist.

*A complex Martini from Harry Craddock. The
additional bitters make this the perfect digestive
cocktail for gin lovers.*

CLOVER CLUB

2 measures gin
¾ measure lemon juice
¾ measure sugar syrup
5 raspberries, plus extra to garnish
½ measure egg white

Y

Add all the ingredients to a
cocktail shaker and vigorously 'dry
shake' without ice for 10 seconds.

Take the shaker apart, add cubed
ice and shake vigorously.

Strain into a coupette glass and
garnish with raspberries.

*Named after the Philadelphia Gentleman's club where it was
first created in the 1800s, this is a sharp pre-Prohibition gin
sour enlivened by raspberries.*

TOM COLLINS

2 measures gin
1 measure lemon juice
¾ measure sugar syrup
soda, to top
to garnish:
lemon and a cocktail cherry

Y

Pour the gin, lemon, sugar syrup
and a splash of soda water into a
highball glass.

Fill the glass with cubed ice and
stir, top with soda and more ice
and garnish with a lemon wedge
and a cocktail cherry.

*First appearing in print in Jerry Thomas's The Bartender's
Guide (1876), yet most likely much older, the classic Tom
Collins is so-named because the original recipe would have
called for 'Old Tom' gin, a sweeter style of gin than London
Dry. Timeless, refreshing and elegant.*

CORPSE REVIVER NO. 2

1 measure gin
1 measure lemon juice
1 measure Lillet Blanc
1 measure Cointreau
2 drops absinthe
lemon, to garnish

Y

Add all the ingredients to a
cocktail shaker filled with
cubed ice.

Shake vigorously and double
strain into a chilled coupette glass.

Garnish with a lemon twist.

*According to its creator (Harry Craddock) 'four of
these taken in quick succession will unrevive the corpse
again.' Start with one and see how you go.*

1900
-1920

LUIGI

2 measures gin
1 measure dry vermouth
½ measure Cointreau
1 measure grenadine
1 measure orange juice
blood orange, to garnish

$\Y$

Add all the ingredients to a
cocktail shaker filled with
cubed ice.

Stir for 30 seconds, and strain
into a chilled cocktail glass.

Garnish with a blood orange twist.

*Created in the early 1900s by Luigi Naintré at the
Embassy Club, London, the Luigi is sweet, sharp and
a touch floral all at once.*

BRONX

2 measures gin
¼ measure sweet vermouth
¼ measure dry vermouth
1 measure orange juice
to garnish:
cocktail cherry and orange

Υ

Add all the ingredients to a
cocktail shaker filled with
cubed ice.

Shake vigorously and double
strain into a chilled coupette glass.

Garnish with a cocktail cherry and
an orange slice.

*A precursor to the Satan's Whiskers, the Bronx first appeared
in print in 1908. It was a hugely popular pre-Prohibition
snifter. In essence, it is a gin Manhattan, freshened with a
splash of orange juice.*

BOBBY BURNS

2 measures Scottish whisky
1 ½ measures sweet vermouth
¼ measure Bénédictine
2 dashes Angostura bitters
lemon, to garnish

Y

Add all the ingredients to a
cocktail shaker filled with
cubed ice.

Stir for 30 seconds, and strain into
a chilled coupette glass.

Garnish with a lemon twist.

*The Bobby Burns is a delicious variant of the Rob Roy
cocktail, itself an interpretation of the Manhattan.
A dash of Bénédictine brings herbal sweetness and
depth of flavour.*

WHITE LADY

1 ½ measures gin
1 measure Cointreau
¾ measure lemon juice
lemon, to garnish

Y

Add all the ingredients to a
cocktail shaker filled with
cubed ice.

Shake vigorously and double
strain into a chilled coupette glass.

Garnish with a lemon twist.

*Essentially a Sidecar made with gin, argument raged
between Harry McElhone and Harry Craddock as to
who created this evergreen classic.*

FRENCH 75

1 measure gin
½ measure lemon juice
½ measure sugar syrup
chilled Champagne, to top
lemon, to garnish

Y

Add the gin, lemon juice and
sugar syrup to a cocktail shaker
filled with cubed ice.

Shake vigorously and strain into a
Champagne flute.

Top with Champagne and garnish
with a lemon twist.

*Created at Harry's New York Bar in Paris in 1915 and
named after the French field gun, this is as much a
Tom Collins with a Champagne top as it is anything
else. The rapid artillery fire of the bubbles is lovely.*

SINGAPORE SLING

1 measure gin
1 measure Cointreau
½ measure Bénédictine
½ measure cherry brandy
¾ lemon juice
soda water, to top
cocktail cherry, to garnish

Y

Add all the ingredients except the
soda water to a cocktail shaker
filled with cubed ice.

Shake vigorously and strain into
a hurricane glass filled with
cubed ice.

Garnish with a cocktail cherry.

*Created at the Raffles Hotel in Singapore in the early 1900s,
this is paradise in a glass. Over the years, pineapple juice has
crept into the recipe and while perfectly permissible, the recipe
here is closer to the original.*

1920S

SOUTHSIDE

2 measures gin

¾ measure lime juice

¾ measure sugar syrup

6 mint leaves

mint, to garnish

$\math020Y$

Add all the ingredients to
a cocktail shaker filled with
cubed ice.

Shake vigorously and double
strain into a chilled coupette glass.

Garnish with a mint leaf.

'Scarface' attained notoriety as the boss of the Chicago Outfit.
His gang imported vast quantities of gin into Chicago's South
side. The gin was poorly made, 'bathtub gin' and flavourings
and sweeteners were required to mask its rough edges. Capone
was partial to a Southside – a fresh, lively and limey cocktail
that could mask all the evils of the world.

GIMLET

2 ½ measures gin
½ measure lime cordial
½ measure lime juice
lime, to garnish

Y

Add all the ingredients to
a cocktail shaker filled with
cubed ice.

Shake vigorously and double
strain into a chilled coupette glass.

Garnish with a lime twist.

*The recipe for the Gimlet varies from source to source
with Raymond Chandler calling for just lime cordial,
others for fresh lime and a touch of sugar syrup. Here,
we've attempted a compromise.*

BEES KNEES

2 measures gin
1 measure lemon juice
½ measure honey

Y

Add all the ingredients to
a cocktail shaker filled with
cubed ice.

Shake vigorously and
double strain into a chilled
coupette glass.

No garnish.

*Literally 'the best', the addition of honey to this
Prohibition-era favourite was a creative method of
masking the dubious taste of poor quality gin. Floral,
zingy and (if made correctly) extremely well balanced.*

MONKEY GLAND

2 measures gin

1 measure orange juice

1 tablespoon Grenadine

2 drops Absinthe (or Pernod)

lemon, to garnish

Y

Add all the ingredients to
a cocktail shaker filled with
cubed ice.

Shake vigorously and strain into a
chilled coupette glass.

Garnish with a lemon twist.

*Here's a MacElhone classic that came straight out of
Harry's New York Bar, Paris in the 1920s.*

HANKY PANKY

2 measures gin
1 measure sweet vermouth
1 tablespoon Fernet-Branca
cocktail cherry, to garnish

🍸

Add all the ingredients to a
cocktail shaker filled with
cubed ice.

Stir for 30 seconds, and strain
into a chilled cocktail glass.

Garnish with cocktail cherries.

---

*This is a subtle twist on the Martinez cocktail, created
by Ada Coleman at the Savoy Hotel, London, in the
early 1900s. Fernet-Branca is an intensely bitter
Italian amaro, and cuts through the sweetness of the
vermouth superbly. Worth a try.*

NEGRONI

1 measure gin
1 measure Campari
1 measure sweet vermouth
orange, to garnish

Y

Pour all the ingredients into a
rocks glass filled with ice.

Stir briefly, and garnish with an
orange slice.

*Though arguably an acquired taste – at least initially
– the intense and bitter complexity of the Negroni is an
unrivalled pleasure.*

BOULEVARDIER

1 ½ measures bourbon

1 measure sweet vermouth

1 measure Campari

orange, to garnish

Y

Fill an old fashioned glass with
cubed ice, and add all
the ingredients.

Stir for 10 seconds and garnish
with an orange twist.

*Essentially a Negroni made with whiskey instead of
gin, the original recipe dates back to Harry's New York
Bar, Paris, in the 1920s. Simple, but utterly delicious.*

OLD PAL

1 ½ measures rye whiskey
¾ measure dry vermouth
½ measure Campari
lemon, to garnish

Y

Add all the ingredients to a
cocktail shaker filled with
cubed ice.

Stir for 30 seconds and strain into
a chilled cocktail glass.

Garnish with a lemon twist.

*A bracing dry Manhattan, with a strong bitter
element provided by Campari. Said to have originated
in Paris in the 1920s at Harry's New York Bar.*

SIDECAR

2 measures cognac

1 measure Cointreau

1 measure lemon juice

lemon, to garnish

Y

Add all the ingredients to a
cocktail shaker filled with
cubed ice.

Shake vigorously and
double strain into a chilled
coupette glass.

Garnish with a lemon twist.

*A Sidecar is a classic 1920s cocktail but its origin is widely
debated. The Ritz Hotel in Paris, London's Buck's Club
and Harry's New York Bar in Paris have all claimed to be
the inventors of this Prohibition-era classic.*

HEMINGWAY DAIQUIRI

1 ¾ measures light rum
¾ measure Maraschino
1 measure lime juice
1 measure grapefruit juice
2 teaspoons sugar syrup
lime wedge, to garnish

🍸

Add all the ingredients to a
cocktail shaker filled with
cubed ice.

Shake vigorously and double
strain into a chilled coupette glass.

Garnish with a lime wedge.

*Created at Floridita in Havana for erstwhile barfly Ernest
Hemingway, the Hemingway Daiquiri is lip-curlingly
sour, so do add a touch more sugar if you wish.*

DEATH IN THE AFTERNOON

½ measure absinthe
chilled Champagne, to top

Υ

Pour the absinthe into the bottom
of a Champagne flute, then
carefully add the Champagne.

No garnish.

A favourite of Ernest Hemingway's, though to suggest
Hemingway had a favourite anything when it came
to drinking possibly belies his zeal for the pastime.
Approach this one with caution.

BUCKS FIZZ

2 measures chilled fresh
orange juice
4 measures chilled Champagne

Y

Add half the Champagne to a
Champagne flute, then carefully
add the orange juice and the rest
of the Champagne.

*Said to be created in 1921 at the Buck's Club in
London, the key to this simple aperitif is using
freshly squeezed orange juice.*

HANGMAN'S BLOOD

2 measures gin

2 measures whisky

2 measures dark rum

2 measures port

2 measures brandy

1 small bottle of stout

Champagne, to top

Y

Add all of the ingredients to
a pint glass and then pour in
the stout.

Top with Champagne.

Anthony Burgess insists this (his own take on the 1929 recipe)
'tastes very smooth, induces a somewhat metaphysical elation,
and rarely leaves a hangover.' We implore you to drink responsibly.

ZOMBIE

1 ½ measures light rum
1 ½ measures dark rum
½ measure Velvet Falernum
½ measure overproof rum
¾ measure lime juice
½ measure grenadine
2 measures grapefruit juice
2 dashes absinthe
1 dash Angostura bitters
mint, to garnish

Y

Add all the ingredients to a cocktail
shaker filled with cubed ice, shake
vigorously and strain into a hurricane
glass (or tiki mug if you have one) filled
with crushed ice.

Garnish with a mint sprig.

*This Tiki classic is a clever blend of fruit that masks
the ludicrous potency of this benchmark rum punch.*

1930S

MAIDEN'S BLUSH

1 ½ measures gin
1 measure orange curaçao
½ measure lemon juice
2 teaspoons grenadine
2 teaspoons sugar syrup
lemon, to garnish

Y

Add all the ingredients to a
cocktail shaker filled with
cubed ice.

Shake vigorously and strain into a
chilled coupette glass.

Garnish with a lemon twist.

A classic from The Savoy Cocktail Book *(1930) by
Harry Craddock, bright and elegant.*

AVIATION

1 ¾ measures gin
½ measure lemon juice
¼ measure Maraschino
¼ measure Crème de Violette
cocktail cherry, to garnish

Y

Add all the ingredients to a
cocktail shaker filled with
cubed ice.

Shake vigorously and double
strain into a chilled coupette glass.

Garnish with a cocktail cherry.

*This is a Harry Craddock classic created at the
Savoy Hotel and first appearing in print in 1930.
The Aviation is another of its creator's endless and
innovative variations on the gin sour – gin is elegantly
balanced with lemon, bitter cherry and perfumed
violet. Easy when you know how.*

SATAN'S WHISKERS

1 ½ measures gin
½ measure orange curaçao
½ measure sweet vermouth
½ measure dry vermouth
1 ½ measures orange juice
2 dashes orange bitters

🍸

Add all the ingredients to a
cocktail shaker filled with
cubed ice.

Shake vigorously and double
strain into a chilled coupette glass.

No garnish.

Conceived by Harry Craddock and first published in The
Savoy Cocktail Book *(1930), this is a richer take on the
Bronx cocktail, wickedly named and sharp to the taste.*

BOXCAR

caster sugar

1 ¾ measures gin

1 measure Cointreau

½ measure lime juice

½ measure sugar syrup

2 teaspoons grenadine

1 egg white

Y

Dip the rim of a chilled coupette
glass in a little lime juice and then
in a small plate of caster sugar to
create a sugar frosting.

Then, add all the ingredients to
a cocktail shaker without ice and
'dry shake' for 10 seconds.

Take the shaker apart, add ice, and
shake again vigorously, and strain into
the prepared coupette glass.

*Somewhere between the White Lady and the Southside
– two classics of the pre-Prohibition and Prohibition
eras, this is a perky and elegant gin sour.*

PERFECT LADY

1 ½ measures gin
¾ measure lemon juice
½ measure peach liqueur
½ measure egg white

Y

Add all the ingredients to a
cocktail shaker and vigorously 'dry
shake' without ice for 10 seconds.

Take the shaker apart, add cubed
ice and shake vigorously.

Double strain into a chilled
coupette glass, no garnish.

*An elegant and floral gin sour perfumed with peach. Created
at the Grosvenor House Hotel in 1936 by Sidney Cox, this is a
sublime and under appreciated classic.*

OPERA

2 measures gin
1 measure Dubonnet
¼ measure Maraschino
orange, to garnish

Y

Add all the ingredients to a
cocktail shaker filled with
cubed ice.

Stir for 30 seconds, and strain into
a chilled cocktail glass.

Garnish with an orange twist.

Dubonnet brings a pleasant richness to this classic
from The Savoy Cocktail Book *(1930).*

GIBSON
MARTINI

2 ½ measures gin
½ measure dry vermouth
cocktail onions, to garnish

Y

Add all the ingredients to a
cocktail shaker filled with
cubed ice.

Stir for 30 seconds, and strain into
a chilled cocktail glass.

Garnish generously with
cocktail onions.

*The Gibson Martini is a classic gin Martini, with an
onion garnish rather than an olive or lemon twist –
which gives a pleasingly unusual acidity.*

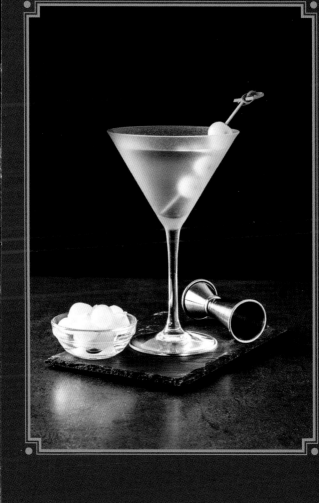

DIRTY MARTINI

2 ½ measures vodka
¼ measure dry vermouth
½ measure olive brine
olives, to garnish

Y

Add all the ingredients to a
cocktail shaker filled with
cubed ice.

Stir for 30 seconds, and strain into
a chilled cocktail glass.

Garnish with olives.

*Apparently a creation of none other than President
Franklin Delano Roosevelt – the dry saltiness of the
Dirty Martini is loathed and loved in equal measure,
depending on the drinker's feelings about olives.*

CHURCHILL
MARTINI

2 measures Plymouth gin
cocktail olive to garnish
(1 bottle of vermouth, to observe)

Y

Add gin to a cocktail shaker filled
with cubed ice and stir briefly.

While stirring glance occasionally
at a bottle of vermouth from across
the room.

Pour into a chilled glass.

Garnish with a single cocktail olive.

*A quirky and complicated man, Winston Churchill
was known for his love of a tipple. When asked how he
would like his gin Martini prepared he replied
'I would like to observe the vermouth from across the
room while I drink my martini.'*

QUEEN MOTHER

2 measures Dubonnet
1 measure gin
lemon, to garnish

Y

Add all the ingredients to an old
fashioned glass filled with cubed
ice, stir briefly and garnish with a
lemon slice.

*'I think that I will take two small bottles of Dubonnet
and gin with me this morning, in case it is needed' once
noted Elizabeth Bowes-Lyons, before taking a trip.
An excellent idea.*

PARADISE

1 ¾ measures gin
½ measure apricot brandy
1 ½ measures orange juice
2 dashes orange bitters
orange, to garnish

Y

Add all the ingredients to a
cocktail shaker filled with
cubed ice.

Shake vigorously and strain into a
coupette glass.

Garnish with an orange twist.

A classic from The Savoy Cocktail Book *(1930),
and yet another riff on the Southside. Tricky to
balance correctly, but worth the effort! Make sure you
use freshly squeezed orange juice.*

GOLDEN DAWN

1 measure gin

1 measure calvados

1 measure apricot brandy

1 ½ measures orange juice

2 teaspoons grenadine

2 dashes Angostura bitters

lemon, to garnish

$\bar{Y}$

Add all the ingredients except the grenadine to a cocktail shaker filled with cubed ice.

Shake vigorously and strain into a coupette glass.

Carefully add the grenadine to create a 'sunrise' effect.

Garnish with a lemon twist.

Hailing from 1930s London, this sharp and fruity snifter doesn't disappoint.

STINGER

2 measures Cognac
½ measure crème de menthe

Y

Add all the ingredients to a
cocktail shaker filled with
cubed ice.

Shake vigorously and double
strain into a chilled cocktail glass.

No garnish.

*A 'stinging', mint-laced cocktail from Harry Craddock,
first published in* The Savoy Cocktail Book *(1930).
It was apparently popular with US Airmen but
whether that was before or after missions is unclear.*

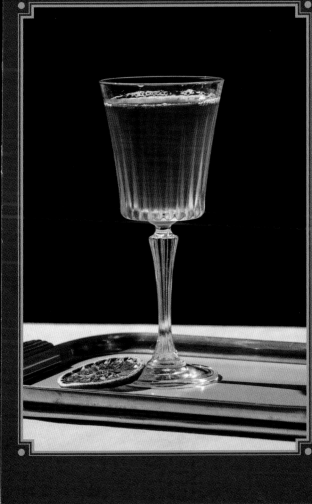

BLOOD
AND SAND

1 measure Scottish whisky
1 measure sweet vermouth
1 measure cherry brandy
1 measure orange juice (freshly squeezed)
orange, to garnish

Y

Add all the ingredients to a
cocktail shaker filled with
cubed ice.

Stir briefly and strain into a
chilled cocktail glass.

Garnish with an orange twist.

*One of the few classic cocktails to feature Scotch, this
is sweet, strong and sacrilegious (to some).*

MINT JULEP

2 measures bourbon
2 teaspoons sugar syrup
8 mint leaves
3 dashes Angostura bitters
mint sprigs, to garnish

Y

Add all the ingredients to a rocks
glass (or Julep cup if you have one)
filled with crushed ice.

Churn vigorously, top with more
crushed ice and garnish with 2–3
mint sprigs.

*This southern United States classic was the official
drink of the Kentucky Derby in the 1930s, Juleps have
been sipped for medicinal purposes for centuries.
A sort of Whiskey Mojito, this is a celebration drink to
get dressed up for on a summer afternoon.*

BLINKER

2 measures rye whiskey

1 measure pink
grapefruit juice

½ measure grenadine

lemon, to garnish

🍸

Add all the ingredients to a
cocktail shaker filled with
cubed ice.

Shake vigorously and double
strain into a chilled coupette glass.

Garnish with a lemon twist.

*First recorded in 1934, the Blinker was something of
a rarity for the time by using grapefruit juice as an
ingredient. Spice from the rye and bitterness from
the grapefruit are balanced by the fruity sweetness
of grenadine.*

ALGONQUIN

1 ¾ measures rye whiskey
½ measure dry vermouth
1 measure pineapple juice
cocktail cherry, to garnish

Y

Add all the ingredients to a
cocktail shaker filled with
cubed ice.

Shake vigorously and double
strain into a chilled coupette glass.

Garnish with a cocktail cherry.

A fantastic whiskey snifter with a tropical twist.
Named after the notorious hotel in mid-town
Manhattan, where it was first served in the 1930s.

BAR
BASICS

WHAT MAKES A GOOD COCKTAIL?

Good cocktails, like good food, are based around quality ingredients. As with cooking, using fresh and homemade ingredients can often make the huge difference between a good drink and an outstanding drink. All of these can be found in department stores, online or in kitchen shops.

$$\mathsf{Y}$$

Ice: You'll need lots of it! Purchase good quality clear ice (the bigger the cubes, the better). If you're hosting a big party, it may be worthwhile finding if you have a local ice supplier that supplies catering companies, as this can be much more cost-effective.

Citrus juice: It's important to use fresh citrus juice in your drinks. Store your fruit out of the refrigerator at room temperature. Look for a soft-skinned fruit for juicing, which you can do with a juicer or citrus press. You can keep fresh citrus juice for a couple of days in the refrigerator, sealed to prevent oxidation.

Sugar syrup: You can buy sugar syrup or you can make your own. The most basic form of sugar syrup is made by mixing caster sugar and hot water together, and stirring until the sugar has dissolved.

The key when preparing sugar syrups is to use a 1:1 ratio of sugar to liquid. White sugar acts as a flavour enhancer, while dark sugars have unique, more toffee flavours and work well with dark spirits.

BASIC SUGAR
SYRUP RECIPE

(Makes 1 litre (1 ¾ pints)
of sugar syrup)

Dissolve 1 kg (2 lb) caster
sugar in 1 litre (1 ¾ pints)
of hot water.

Allow to cool.

Y

Sugar syrup will keep in a sterilized bottle stored in the refrigerator for up to two weeks.

USEFUL EQUIPMENT

Y

Shaker: The Boston shaker is the most simple option, but it needs to be used in conjunction with a Hawthorne strainer. Alternatively you could choose a shaker with a built-in strainer.

Hawthorne strainer: This type of strainer is often used in conjunction with a Boston shaker, but a simple tea strainer will also work well.

Measure or jigger: Single and double measures are available and are essential when you are mixing ingredients so that the proportions are always the same. One measure is 25 ml or 1 fl oz.

Mixing glass: A mixing glass is used for those drinks that require only a gentle stirring before they are poured or strained.

Bar spoon: Similar to a teaspoon but with a long handle, a bar spoon is used for stirring, layering and muddling drinks.

Muddling stick: Similar to a pestle, which will work just as well, a muddling stick, or muddler, is used to crush fruit or herbs in a glass or shaker for drinks like the Mojito.

Food processor: A food processor or blender is useful for making frozen cocktails and smoothies.

TECHNIQUES

Shaking: Shaking mixes ingredients thoroughly and quickly, and chills the drink before serving.

> Fill a cocktail shaker with ice cubes, or cracked or crushed ice. If the recipe calls for a chilled glass add a few ice cubes and some cold water to the glass, swirl it around and discard. Add the ingredients to the shaker and shake until a frost forms on the outside. Strain the cocktail into the glass and then serve.

Stirring: Stirring mixes and chills drinks, but also maintains their clarity. Add the ingredients to a glass, in recipe order. Use a bar spoon to stir the drink, lightly or vigorously, as described in the recipe. Finish the drink with any decoration and serve.

Double-straining: To prevent all traces of puréed fruit and ice fragments from entering the glass, use a shaker with a built-in strainer in conjunction with a Hawthorne strainer. A fine strainer also works well.

Muddling: A technique used to bring out the flavours of herbs and fruit using a blunt tool called a muddler. Add chosen herb(s) to a highball glass. Add some sugar syrup and some lime wedges.

Hold the glass firmly and use a muddler or pestle to twist and press down. Continue for 30 seconds, top up with crushed ice and add remaining ingredients.

Blending: Be careful not to add too much ice as this will dilute the cocktail. It's best to add a little at a time.

Layering: Some spirits can be served layered on top of each other – the more viscous or sugary the liquid, the heavier it will be. Pour the heaviest liquid into a glass, taking care that it does not touch the sides. Position a bar spoon in the centre of the glass, rounded part down and facing you. Rest the spoon against the side of the glass as you pour the next heaviest ingredient down the spoon. It should float on top of the first liquid. Follow step 2, with the lightest ingredient at the top.

The measure that has been used in the recipes is based on a bar jigger, which is 25 ml (1 fl oz). If preferred, a different volume can be used, providing the proportions are kept consistent within a drink and suitable adjustments are made to spoon measurements, where they occur.

Standard level spoon measurements are used in all recipes.

1 tablespoon = one 15 ml spoon
1 teaspoon = one 5 ml spoon

This book contains cocktails made with raw or lightly cooked eggs. It is prudent for more vulnerable people to avoid uncooked or lightly cooked cocktails made with eggs.